WAFFEN SS IN RUSSIA

Disabled Tiger I – but what a
lovely shot! (458/77/16).

BRUCE QUARRIE
WAFFEN SS IN RUSSIA

WORLD WAR 2 PHOTO ALBUM NUMBER 3

A selection of German wartime photographs
from the Bundesarchiv, Koblenz

PSL Patrick Stephens, Cambridge

First published in 1978

British Library Cataloguing in Publication Data
Waffen-SS in Russia. –
    (World War 2 photo albums; 3).
    1. Nationalsozialistische Deutsche
    Arbeiter-Partei.
    Schutzstaffel. Waffenschutzstaffel – Pictorial
    works. 2. World War,1939–1945 – Campaigns
    – Russia – Pictorial works
    I. Quarrie, Bruce II. Series
    940.54'21   D764

    ISBN 0 85059 340 9 (casebound)
    ISBN 0 85059 317 4 (softbound)

Design by Tim McPhee

Photoset in 10pt Plantin Roman. Printed in Great
Britain on 100 gsm Pedigree coated cartridge and
bound by The Garden City Press Limited,
Letchworth, Hertfordshire, SG6 1JS, for the
publishers, Patrick Stephens Limited, Bar Hill,
Cambridge, CB3 8EL.

CONTENTS

Acknowledgements
The author and publisher would like to express their sincere thanks to Dr Matthias Haupt and Herr Meinrad Nilges of the Bundesarchiv for their assistance, without which this book would have been impossible.

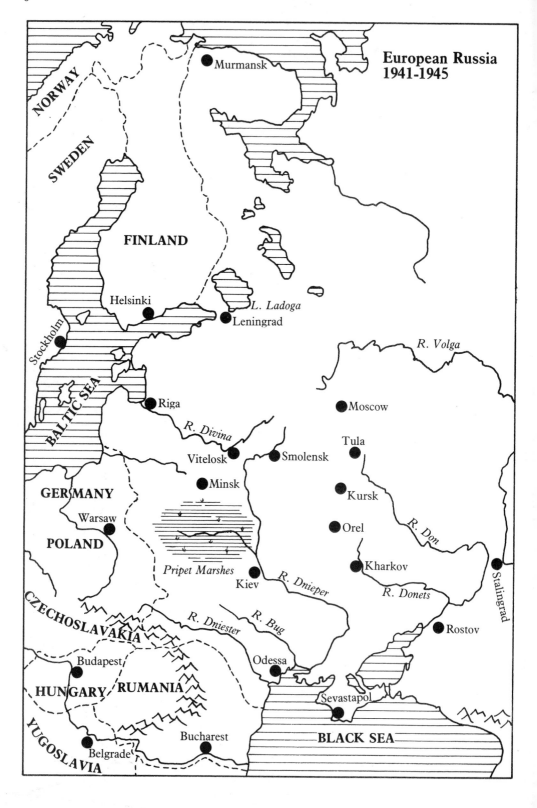

European Russia 1941-1945

NORWAY

SWEDEN

FINLAND

Murmansk

Helsinki

Stockholm

L. Ladoga

Leningrad

R. Volga

BALTIC SEA

Riga

R. Divina

Moscow

GERMANY

Vitelosk

Smolensk

Tula

Warsaw

Minsk

Kursk

POLAND

Orel

R. Don

Pripet Marshes

Kiev

R. Dnieper

Kharkov

R. Donets

Stalingrad

CZECHOSLOVAKIA

R. Dniester

R. Bug

Rostov

Budapest

Odessa

HUNGARY

RUMANIA

Sevastapol

YUGOSLAVIA

Bucharest

BLACK SEA

Belgrade

When Hitler invaded Soviet Russia in June 1941, Waffen-SS divisions were in the forefront of the fighting and remained there throughout the war, spearheading the drive on Moscow and the battles around Kharkov and Kursk, and finally capitulating only after last-ditch stands in the crumbling ruins of the Third Reich in 1945. Throughout these four years the SS divisions, whose personnel owed their loyalty personally to Hitler rather than to the German state, and whom he therefore trusted more than the Army, were placed wherever the situation was most critical and the fighting hardest. Their casualties were enormous, but their loyalty immense.

Volunteers for the Waffen-SS were enlisted through the ordinary Army recruiting offices who, naturally, did not want to see the cream of German youth entering 'Himmler's private army' and held their numbers down to a mere third of what they might otherwise have been. Nevertheless, by 1944 there were approximately 910,000 fighting soldiers in some 38 SS divisions – not all stationed in Russia, of course. In 1941, however, there were only four divisions involved: the SS Leibstandarte 'Adolf Hitler', the SS 'Reich' (later to be renamed 'Das Reich'), the SS 'Totenkopf' and the SS 'Wiking'. The first and last of these formed part of von Kleist's Panzergruppe in Army Group South, SS 'Reich' as part of Guderian's Panzergruppe in the centre, and 'Totenkopf' as part of Hoepner's Panzergruppe in the north. At this time the SS formations were of similar composition and strength to regular Army motorised infantry divisions, but included a small complement of tanks. Later in the war they were to grow to the size of full-fledged Panzer divisions.

These four divisions were later augmented by the SS-Polizei Panzer-Grenadier Division, the SS Gebirgs (Mountain) Division 'Nord', the SS Kavallerie-Division 'Florian Geyer', the SS Panzer Divisions 'Hohenstaufen', 'Frundsberg' and 'Hitler Jugend', the SS Panzer-Grenadier Divisions 'Reichführer-SS' and 'Götz von Berlichingen'; various Volksdeutsch divisions (eg, SS Freiwilligen-Gebirgs Division 'Prinz Eugen' and Panzer-Grenadier Division 'Horst Wessel'); and a number of divisions constituted from foreign volunteers, including French, Hungarian, Croatian, Dutch, Italian and Russian troops. In addition, there were several smaller, semi-independent SS units, such as Fallschirmjäger, Nebelwerfer and heavy tank battalions.

Waffen-SS troops were dressed and equipped similarly to Army personnel but with special distinctions. Instead of tricolour and eagle decals, their helmets bore the SS runes and a swastika. In place of a tricolour button, their caps bore a white metal 'Totenkopf' (death's head) device. Their national eagle was different, having the tips of the wings shaped into a 'V' rather than a wedge shape, and it was worn on the upper left sleeve of their uniform jackets instead of on the right breast. Their collar patches were black lozenges with rank distinctions on the left and SS runes on the right (the exception being SS Division 'Totenkopf', which wore death's head symbols). Their shoulder straps were black instead of field grey but otherwise followed the Army system of rank distinctions. Belt buckles were similar to Army ones but bore the SS motto 'Meine Ehre heisst Treue!' (Loyalty is my Honour) instead of 'Gott mit Uns'. Trousers and boots were the same as in the Army, as was tropical kit (although many SS units favoured the Luftwaffe-style tropical uniform instead).

In the field, the major difference between SS and Army troops lay in their camouflage smocks. The Waffen-SS developed camouflage to a fine art, and in place of the ordinary Army reversible white/splinter camouflage version had a variety of patterns in spring, summer, autumn and winter colours designed to blend in with virtually any landscape. This system extended to helmet covers and, later, trousers, although the original camouflage smock was a simple, loose, elasticated or draw-stringed affair. Camouflaged one- and two-piece AFV crew uniforms were also issued as the war progressed as an alternative to the normal Panzer black or field grey short double-breasted jacket and trousers worn respectively by tank and self-propelled gun crews. 'Waffenfarbe', or arm of service colour, was basically the same as in the Army, with a couple of exceptions – for example, Panzer-Grenadiers in the SS wore white instead of green, and anti-tank gunners Panzer pink instead of artillery red. During the Russian winter Waffen-SS troops received the same reversible white/mouse grey blanket-lined clothing as the Army, although during the winter of 1942 some units received special issue parkas. Rank distinctions on camouflage clothing took the form of a system of green or yellow bars and oakleaves worn on the upper left sleeve, similar to the bars and wings worn on Fallschirmjäger jump smocks. Finally, many SS formations wore special distinguishing armbands giving the unit name on their lower left sleeves.*

SS weapons and equipment, contrary to popular belief, were identical to those issued to the Army, although it is true that, towards the end of the war, their tank battalions were stronger by approximately 20 per cent. The regular infantry weapon was the Kar 98K carbine, supplemented by MP 40 submachine-guns, MG 34 and MG 42 machine-guns, the MP 43 assault rifle and mortars of 5 cm, 8.1 cm and 12 cm calibres. There was a higher proportion of automatic and heavy weapons in the Panzer and Panzer-Grenadier formations which has contributed to the false impression that the Waffen-SS were better equipped than the Army. In fact the only real difference was that the élite SS Panzer-Grenadier regiments had a full complement of armoured half-tracks whereas most Army Panzer-Grenadier regiments only had half. In addition, SS Panzer divisions included a Nebelwerfer Abteilung (battalion).

Tanks and AFVs used by the Waffen-SS in Russia included the PzKpfw III in 1941, the PzKpfw IV in progressively up-armoured and up-gunned versions throughout the war, the PzKpfw VI Tiger I from 1942 onwards, the PzKpfw V Panther from 1943, and the PzKpfw VI Tiger II in the closing stages of the war; the StuG III assault gun in all its various guises; the Jagdpanzer IV, Jagdpanther and Hetzer; Marder Is, IIs and IIIs; the Nashorn, Hummel and Wespe;

and SdKfz 250 and 251 armoured half-tracks. Once again, most of these are illustrated and identified in various photographs.

The SS divisions began life as battalions, were later expanded to the size of regiments, then divisions. They were motorised, refitted as Panzer-Grenadier divisions for the most part, and some finally as Panzer divisions. Their earliest AFVs were StuG IIIs, self-propelled guns on the PzKpfw III tank chassis with armoured superstructures housing a variety of weapons: long- and short-barrelled 7.5 cm guns and 10.5 cm howitzers. Their armour plate varied from 20 to 80 mm, they weighed between 22 and 24 tons, carried a crew of four, had a top speed of 25 mph and an average range of 80 miles.

These assault guns were soon supplemented by PzKpfw III tanks, which had similar performance figures but a crew of five and mounted 3.7 or 5 cm guns. By the time of the invasion of Russia, however, the PzKpfw III was on the way out, and the PzKpfw IV took its place for the remainder of the war as the 'workhorse' of all German Panzer divisions. The PzKpfw IV was a versatile machine weighing 20 to 25 tons depending on armament and armour. It carried a crew of five, had armour thickness varying from 20 to 80 mm, and mounted a variety of guns, the most successful of which was the long-barrelled 7.5 cm KwK 40 L/48. Later variants of the PzKpfw IV featured spaced turret armour and side skirts as protection against hollow-charge anti-tank weapons. The vehicle had a maximum speed of 25 mph and an average range of 103 miles. As the war progressed, the PzKpfw IV was largely supplemented by the PzKpfw V Panther, considered by some the finest tank design of the war. Copied to a large extent from the Russian T-34, the Panther featured well-sloped armour plate of 40 to 110 mm thickness, mounted a 7.5 cm KwK 42 L/70 gun, carried a crew of five, had a top speed of just under 30 mph and an average range of 80 miles.

Appearing out of numerical sequence before the Panther was the PzKpfw VI Tiger I, a massive, heavy and slow tank which was virtually indestructible and which carried a version of the famous German 8.8 cm anti-aircraft gun as its main armament, the KwK 36 L/56 which could fire eight rounds a minute and penetrate some 95 mm of armour plate at an effective range of around 1,500 yards: adequate to knock out any Russian tank with the exception of the JS series with

* This is, of necessity, a very brief and incomplete description of SS clothing, but many examples can be seen in the photographs and, for further detail, readers are recommended to one of the many specialist books on this subject. A good and inexpensive introduction is Walther-Karl Holzmann's *Manual of the Waffen-SS*, published by Argus Books in 1976.

relative impunity. The Tiger I carried a crew of five, weighed 55 tons, had armour thickness varying between 80 and 100 mm, a top speed of 24 mph and an average range of 50 miles. Its successor was the Tiger II, or Königs Tiger, similar in design to the Panther but weighing over 69 tons and mounting the long-barrelled, high-velocity 8.8 cm KwK 43 L/71 gun. Although only produced in relatively small quantities, this was the most powerful tank of the war, superior to the Soviet JS 2, but suffered from lack of power and manoeuvrability. It carried a crew of five, had armour thickness ranging from 80 to 185 mm, a top speed of 24 mph and an average range of 61 miles.

The Germans pioneered the use of self-propelled anti-tank guns, or 'Panzerjägers', in Russia. The three most successful types used by the SS were the Jagdpanzer IV, the Jagdpanther and the Hetzer. The Jagdpanzer IV was a low, streamlined design on a PzKpfw IV tank chassis mounting the 7.5 cm StuK 42 L/70 gun. It weighed just under 26 tons and carried a crew of four, with armour plate between 20 and 80 mm thick. It could travel at up to 25 mph and had an average range of 103 miles. The Jagdpanther was unquestionably the most successful SP anti-tank gun of the war, being based on the Panther tank chassis but mounting an 8.8 cm Pak 43/3 L/71 gun in a fixed fighting compartment which accommodated five crewmen. It weighed 45½ tons, had a top speed of 39 mph and an average range of 105 miles. The Hetzer was a small SPG mounted on the obsolete Czech PzKpfw 38(t) chassis carrying a 7.5 cm Pak 39 L/48 gun, a crew of four, and having a top speed and average range of 25 mph and 95 miles respectively. The Jagdpanther featured armour of between 40 and 80 mm thickness, the Hetzer a mere eight to 60 mm. But what the Hetzer lacked in weight it made up in manoeuvrability, and still packed a hefty punch.

Less successful than these three SPGs were the Marders, open-topped vehicles mounted on obsolete light tank chassis and carrying 7.5 cm or re-bored Russian 76.2 mm guns; and the Nashorn, a similar vehicle mounting an 8.8 cm gun on a PzKpfw III/IV chassis. Similar in appearance also were the Wespe and Hummel SP howitzers, carrying 10.5 and 15 cm weapons respectively on PzKpfw II and III/IV chassis.

SS Panzer and Panzer-Grenadier divisions were widely equipped also with SdKfz 250 and 251 half-tracks, the former predominantly in a reconnaissance and the latter in a troop-carrying role. These lightly armoured vehicles enabled the infantry grenadiers to keep up with the tanks and afforded them some protection from small-arms fire and shrapnel, although their narrow tracks did not give good purchase over soft ground.

Waffen-SS AFVs were painted in the same camouflage colours as Army vehicles. Up to 1942 the standard colour was a dark grey, but after this all vehicles leaving the factories were finished in a dark sandy yellow, over which camouflage patterns in red/brown and dark green could be painted by individual units. During the Russian winter, most vehicles were more or less thoroughly whitewashed. Three-digit call-sign numbers appeared on the turret sides of tanks and on the hull sides of SPGs and half-tracks, usually in black or dark red outlined white. Divisional and tactical identifying symbols in yellow or white commonly, but far from universally, appeared on the front and rear plates of AFVs; they were more systematically applied to 'soft-skin' vehicles where camouflage was less important. Number plates were prefixed by SS runes instead of 'WH' (Army) or 'WL' (Luftwaffe). Finally, a large number of unofficial slogans and names appeared, including girlfriend's or wife's names, above the driver's visor, around the commander's cupola or on the upper hull sides. Red, white and black swastika flags were frequently draped across the most convenient flat horizontal surfaces of vehicles as an aerial recognition device – fair enough in Russia where the Luftwaffe was so powerful, but something which rapidly fell into disfavour in Italy and Normandy! As the war progressed, increasing numbers of tanks had 'zimmerit' paste applied to all flat surfaces. This was a form of paste which prevented magnetic mines and other hollow-charge armour-piercing devices from adhering to the vehicle.

There is only space here to describe Waffen-SS operations in Russia in the briefest terms, and I have therefore restricted most of my remarks to the four cadre divisions, Leibstandarte 'Adolf Hitler', 'Das Reich', 'Totenkopf' and 'Wiking'. The SS Panzer Division 'Hohenstaufen' was only operational in the east from April to June 1944 and 'Frundsberg' from March to June of the same year. 'Hitler Jugend' served exclusively in the west until January 1945 when it was transferred to Hungary. Of the Panzer-Grenadier divisions, only the 'Polizei' fought extensively in Russia, most of the remainder being present for just a few months in 1944–1945. The Gebirgs Division 'Nord' and the SS Cavalry Division 'Florian Geyer' also saw active service in the East.

The Leibstandarte 'Adolf Hitler', originally formed in 1933, had fought in Poland, France and the Balkans prior to June 1941. During the initial stages of Army Group South's operations it fought with Panzergruppe 'Kleist' in the drive towards the Crimea then, in November 1941, along the coast of the Sea of Azov to Rostov, where it was repelled by a Russian counter-attack. The somewhat mauled unit was posted to France to refit as a Panzer division during the summer of 1942, but rushed back to the east in January 1943 to join 'Das Reich' and 'Totenkopf' in Hausser's 2nd SS Panzer Korps during the desperate fighting for Kharkov. These three SS divisions then spearheaded the German armoured forces in the south during the largest tank battle of the war, at Kursk in the summer of 1943. Unable to make significant headway against the stubborn Soviet resistance, the Germans called the attack off and the Leibstandarte 'AH' was transferred to Italy, but returned to Russia in the autumn. It was encircled during the Soviet winter offensive of 1942–1943 but rescued by the remainder of the 2nd SS Panzer Korps and then sent west again to recoup its heavy losses. During 1944 the division fought in Normandy and the Ardennes offensive, was transferred to Hungary at the beginning of 1945 to meet the strong Russian thrust, and ended the war in Austria, where its commander, 'Sepp' Dietrich, surrendered to the Americans.

The 'Das Reich' Division had also fought in Poland, France and the Balkans although under a different name (SS-VT Division, then SS-V Division, then SS 'Reich'). In June 1941 'Reich', together with the Army's 'Grossdeutschland' Regiment, spearheaded Guderian's drive on Smolensk, and distinguished itself in the bitter fighting around Elnya. It took little part in Guderian's southward thrust to complete the encirclement around Kiev, but was back at the front for the final abortive drive on Moscow through the autumn mud and winter snow. The division was heavily engaged in defensive fighting west of Moscow during the

remainder of the winter before being recalled to France for a refit in March 1942. As recounted, it formed part of Hausser's Panzer Korps during the 1943 battles of Kharkov and Kursk, where it again distinguished itself.

The division helped to extricate the Leibstandarte 'AH' from its encirclement at the beginning of 1944, but then returned to France where it also participated in the heavy Normandy fighting, and was largely instrumental in holding open the 'neck' of the Falaise gap, allowing large numbers of German troops to escape from the converging British and Americans. It also fought in the Ardennes and finished the war in Austria, where it too surrendered to the Americans.

The 'Totenkopf' Division, formed predominantly from former concentration camp guards in 1939, fought in Poland and France and then, in June 1941, was attached to Army Group North for the invasion of Russia. It took part in the triumphant advance through the Baltic States and reached the outskirts of Leningrad, but was trapped in the Demyansk pocket during the Soviet winter counter-offensive, and remained fighting defensively in this sector until the autumn of 1942. Returning to France for a refit, it joined the Leibstandarte 'AH' and 'Das Reich' in early 1943 during the battles for Kharkov and Kursk, after which it remained in defensive positions while its two comrade divisions returned to France. Falling back steadily under the increasing Russian pressure, the division was transferred to Poland in autumn 1944 where, together with the SS Divison 'Wiking', it succeeded in throwing the Russians back from Warsaw and across the River Vistula. These two divisions also participated in the ruthless quashing of the Warsaw uprising, and remained in this sector until the end of 1944, when they were ordered into Hungary to try to break the Russian encirclement of Budapest. Finally, 'Totenkopf' retreated into Austria and surrendered to the Americans, but unluckily the division's troops were handed over to the Russians. Few survived.

The 'Wiking' Division was not formed until December 1940, although one of its parent regiments, 'Germania', had fought in France as part of the SS-V Division. Unlike the three divisions so far described, it included Danish, Norwegian, Dutch and Flemish volunteers in the 'Nordland' and

'Westland' Regiments. It fought in Galicia with Army Group South during the invasion of Russia and succeeded in establishing a bridgehead across the River Dnieper in August 1941. Together with the Leibstandarte 'AH' it reached Rostov but was then pushed back into defensive positions behind the River Mius. During 1942 the division helped spearhead von Kleist's drive towards the Caucasus, and remained on the defensive in this region during the winter of 1942–1943. When the Russians launched their winter counter-offensive, 'Wiking' was one of the divisions entrapped in the Cherkassy pocket where, as the sole armoured unit present, it spearheaded the breakout, though at great loss to itself. Refitted at the beginning of 1944, it fought with 'Totenkopf' in the Warsaw sector and then in the unsuccessful attempt to break the encirclement of Budapest at the beginning of 1945. 'Wiking' finally surrendered to the Russians in Czechoslovakia.

The SS Polizei Panzer-Grenadier Division began its existence in 1939 and was composed of ordinary German policemen in the first instance. Although numbered fourth in the SS divisional table, it was not treated as an élite unit and puts the lie to tales of SS over Army favouritism. For the 1940 campaign in France it was horse-drawn and remained so for the initial stages of Operation 'Barbarossa', the invasion of Russia, where it, along with 'Totenkopf', fought in the north. It differed from the other SS divisions in having the police eagle on the left-hand side of its helmets instead of the swastika shield. Held in reserve during the first month of the campaign, the division lost heavily in August during the fighting around Luga but still participated in the siege of Leningrad and the fierce winter fighting around Lake Ladoga. It fought defensively throughout 1942, was briefly returned to Germany in spring 1943 to be refitted as a Panzer-Grenadier division, and then sent to the Balkans. It ended the war fighting the Russians in the Danzig sector but managed to surrender to the Americans west of the River Elbe in 1945. General officers in this division had police green instead of black backings to their collar patches and shoulder boards.

After initial service in Norway, Kampfgruppe 'Nord' (created from elements of SS 'Totenkopf') was formed into a division in the summer of 1941 and, for the invasion of Russia, sent to join von Falkenhorst's command in Finland. Composed mainly of former policemen with little military training, the division proved unreliable in its initial engagements, and was split up. A new division was established during the winter of 1941–1942 and specifically trained as a mountain unit. In the autumn of 1942 the new troops were united in Finland with the remnants of Kampfgruppe 'Nord', and saw a quiet year on the comparatively tranquil northern front. This ended in the summer of 1944 when the Russians broke through the Finnish lines and imposed a peace with terms which included the removal of German troops from Finnish soil. SS Division 'Nord' was split up, elements arriving in Norway and Denmark, where they were regrouped and sent to assist on the southern sector of the Ardennes offensive of December 1944. Here they achieved little and eventually surrendered to the Americans in Bavaria.

Six very different stories which sum up the Waffen-SS's achievements and failures on the eastern front. The German author Heinz Hoehne makes the following comment: 'The SS soldiers were living in another world, a cruel remorseless world, aeons removed from the ideological verbiage of the SS. Driven by belief in their Führer and in the ultimate victory of Germany, the SS formations stormed through the steppes, marshes and forests of Russia, both heroes and victims of a ghastly chapter of human error and hallucination. They won for themselves a select place in the annals of war. Whether in the south, the centre or the north, wherever the enemy recovered sufficiently from his surprise to stand and fight, wherever he launched a counter-attack and tore gaps in the German attacking front, orders went out for SS formations.'

By this, he means, of course, the élite units. There were many others present in Russia or on the eastern front (eg, in Yugoslavia), including the 'Prinz Eugen' Gebirgsjäger Division which was formed in 1942 and spent most of the war in anti-guerrilla operations; the SS Kavallerie-Division 'Florian Geyer', formed from the original SS Kavallerie-Brigade in 1942 and containing a high percentage of Hungarian recruits, which fought in the centre during 1942 and in the south during 1943, where it suffered heavy casualties; the 'Nordland' Panzer-Grenadier Division, composed mainly of Scandinavian volunteers in 1943, which was also predominantly engaged in anti-partisan warfare; and Armenian, Croatian, Latvian, Estonian, Georgian, Lithuanian, Caucasian, Turkoman, Ukrainian, Tartar and Cossack brigades and divisions. These units strongly reflected the fierce independent spirit of many regions which had been forcibly subjected to Communist rule since the Revolution and which were antipathetic to the Soviet 'cause', although they have subsequently been accounted 'traitors' and harshly treated.

In the early days of the war, there was a strong feeling of rivalry between the SS and regular Army units; as the conflict progressed, however, this soon evaporated and the two 'armies' fought side by side with mutual respect. Rommel distrusted the SS, but as early as 1941 Guderian had nothing but good to say for their courage, morale and discipline – an attitude later expressed in black and white by Manstein and others. SS atrocities have received a great deal of attention, but in fact were often the responsibility of individuals or small units, not of the fighting troops as a whole; and there are few armies in history, including the Allies in 1939–1945, who can declare themselves categorically free of similar actions.

But I did not intend to philosophise. This is a pictorial impression of the Waffen-SS in Russia, and the photographs speak for themselves. I have tried to select a balanced mixture illustrating both SS vehicles and uniforms from 1941 to 1944, in both winter and summer, as well as occasional pictures of specific officers, who can be identified and whose clothing illustrates SS rank badges and insignia. The relatively poor quality of several of the photos is explained in the following footnote. Researching this title was instructive, but the final selection is, of necessity, subjective, and may not include pictures which the individual reader would particularly like to see. This would still be the case if we were to reproduce every single SS picture in the Bundesarchiv!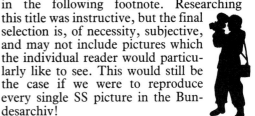

ABOUT THE PHOTOGRAPHS

The photographs in this book have been selected with care from the Bundesarchiv, Koblenz (the approximate German equivalent of the US National Archives or the British Public Records Office). Particular attention has been devoted to choosing photographs which will be fresh to the majority of readers, although it is inevitable that one or two may be familiar. Other than this, the author's prime concern has been to choose good-quality photographs which illustrate the type of detail that enthusiasts and modellers require. In certain instances quality has, to a degree, been sacrificed in order to include a particularly interesting photograph. For the most part, however, the quality speaks for itself.

The Bundesarchiv files hold some one million black and white negatives of Wehrmacht and Luftwaffe subjects, including 150,000 on the Kriegsmarine, some 20,000 glass negatives from the inter-war period and several hundred colour photographs. Sheer numbers is one of the problems which makes the compilation of a book such as this difficult. Other difficulties include the fact that, in the vast majority of cases, the negatives have not been printed so the researcher is forced to look though box after box of 35 mm contact strips – some 250 boxes containing an average of over 5,000 pictures each, plus folders containing a further 115,000 contact prints of the Waffen-SS*; moreover, cataloguing and indexing the negatives is neither an easy nor a short task, with the result that, at the present time, Luftwaffe and Wehrmacht subjects as well as entirely separate theatres of operations are intermingled in the same files.

There is a simple explanation for this confusion. The Bundesarchiv photographs were taken by war correspondents attached to German military units, and the negatives were originally stored in the Reich Propaganda Ministry in Berlin. Towards the close of the Second World War, all the photographs – then numbering some $3\frac{1}{2}$ million – were ordered to be destroyed. One man in the Ministry, a Herr Evers, realised that they should be preserved for posterity and, acting entirely unofficially and on his own initiative, commandeered the first available suitable transport – two refrigerated fish trucks – loaded the negatives into them, and set out for safety. Unfortunately, one of the trucks disappeared en route and, to this day, nobody knows what happened to it. The remainder were captured by the Americans and shipped to Washington, where they remained for 20 years before the majority were returned to the government of West Germany. A large number, however, still reside in Washington. Thus the Bundesarchiv files are incomplete, with infuriating gaps for any researcher. Specifically, they end in the autumn of 1944, after Arnhem, and thus record none of the drama of the closing months of the war.

The photographs are currently housed in a modern office block in Koblenz, overlooking the River Mosel. The priceless negatives are stored in the basement, and there are strict security checks on anyone seeking admission to the Bildarchiv (Photo Archive). Regrettably, and the author has been asked to stress this point, the archives are *only open to bona fide authors and publishers, and prints can only be supplied for reproduction in a book or magazine*. They CANNOT be supplied to private collectors or enthusiasts for personal use, so *please* – don't write to the Bundesarchiv or the publishers of this book asking for copy prints, because they cannot be provided. The well-equipped photo laboratory at the Bundesarchiv is only capable of handling some 80 to 100 prints per day because each is printed individually under strictly controlled conditions – another reason for the fine quality of the photographs but also a contributory factor in the above legislation.

---

* The quality of photographs of the Waffen-SS is not, on the whole, as crisp as that of other subjects, for the very good reason that the original negatives no longer exist and the prints you see in this book are enlarged direct from 35 mm contacts.

THE PHOTOGRAPHS

Left Officers and light car of the 'Totenkopf' Division, summer 1941. Note death's head device on offside mudguard, tactical device denoting the third battalion of a towed artillery regiment, and red and black battalion command pennant on the nearside mudguard (78/22/8).

Right SS infantryman with standard 98K carbine slung across his back. Note typical style of Russian village architecture (78/22/27).

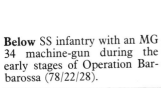

Below SS infantry with an MG 34 machine-gun during the early stages of Operation Barbarossa (78/22/28).

Above The Leibstandarte-SS 'Adolf Hitler' advances into Russia. The tactical device just discernible on the left foreground vehicle, and the gun barrel projecting skywards to its right, suggest an SP anti-tank unit (73/101/41).

Above left SS artillerymen with a 15 cm sIG 33 in 1941 (73/89/30).

Above right Light signals car of the 'Totenkopf' Division displaying a variation of the more normal tactical insignia on its nearside mudguard (78/22/10).

Left Grenadier of the 'Totenkopf' Division in the summer of 1941. He wears one of the special SS camouflage smocks and his belt buckle identifies him as an officer, rank unknown (78/22/9).

Right Traffic jam! Motorcyclists, believed to be of the 'Totenkopf' Division, in Russia. Note SS number plates and tactical signs for the 15th company (or troop?) of a motorised recce unit (left) and motorised recce unit HQ (right) (78/22/7).

18

Left The 'Das Reich' divisional sign can just be seen underneath the tactical device of a motorcycle recce unit on the nearside mudguard of this car, while the white 'G' of Panzergruppe Guderian is clearly visible on the offside. The sign says that the bridge, over the river Desna, was built by Pioneer Battalion 48 (73/85/88).

Right Good portrait shot of an unidentified SS grenadier carrying an MP 28 II sub-machine-gun (73/94/48).

Below left Loading belts of ammunition for an MG 34. Note early pattern SS field caps with offset peak (73/95/18).

Below Grenadiers of an unidentified SS unit interrogate local Russian farmers. The man in the rear seat of the car clasps an MG 34 with bipod LMG mount (73/92/66).

are civilians non-combatants "interrogated" - or only questioned?

Far left HQ units of a towed artillery battalion, SS Division 'Das Reich' (78/22/29).

Left A moment's break for a soldier of the SS Kavallerie Division (73/97/48).

Right The man on the left wears the standard rubberised motor-cycle riding coat while the soldier on the right wears standard side cap with SS eagle, camou-flaged smock, field-grey trousers and black marching boots. Note bayonet and Luger holster (78/22/6).

Below left Local command post set up in a prosperous Russian villager's garden. Note despatch cyclists standing in background (73/82/37).

Below Reconnaissance party, thought to be of the 'Wiking' Division, with an SdKfz 232 armoured car, date unknown (73/87/32).

Inset left Towed Pak 37 anti-tank gun of the 'Totenkopf' Division (73/95/28).

Inset right Late version StuG IIIs with long-barrelled 7.5 cm guns of the 'Totenkopf' Division (78/22/26).

Background photograph 3.7 cm flak gun and detachment from an SS anti-aircraft unit (73/89/24).

Left Men of the SS Kavallerie Division carrying a wounded soldier past an abandoned Russian BA 10 armoured car (73/96/10).

Right SdKfz 261 light radio car of a motorised SS recce unit, possibly 'Totenkopf' Division (78/22/15).

Below left Light car clearly showing the 'Totenkopf' Division's sign (78/22/13).

Below Motorcyclists of the same division showing the more usual version of the 'Totenkopf' device (78/22/14).

Above Pak 37 anti-tank gun being towed along the bed of a stream by men of the 'Totenkopf' Division (77/93/7).

Above Right SS motorcycle unit during a pause in the advance. Note aerial recognition flag draped over the engine covers of the SdKfz 261 (73/82/43).

Left Officer and men of the 'Totenkopf' Division during 1941 (76/90/5).

Right Officers of SS 'Reich' Division. Note tapes on sleeves to hold camouflage foliage (73/135/36).

Above SS gunners with a Pak 37 during the seemingly endless advance (73/95/6).

Above left Men and vehicles of the SS Kavallerie Division in 1941 (73/96/20). Note divisional sword device on the front of the SdKfz 222.

Left Obersturmführer Fegelein (on right), with other men of the SS Kavallerie Division in 1941 (73/96/22).

Right Decorations being awarded to men of the 'Totenkopf' Division by an SS Untersturmführer. They are smartly dressed in standard field-grey tunics and trousers, black marching boots and steel helmets with SS decals. The foreground figure is an NCO (78/22/20).

OVERLEAF

Background photograph Interesting shot of a 'Das Reich' StuG III showing the regimental device of the 'Deutschland' Regiment (596/395/29).

Left inset Would you believe it? PzKpfw IIas actually being used by SS 'Reich' in 1941, as clearly denoted by the white 'G' on the bow plate (78/22/32).

Right inset The date given for this photograph of an SS SdKfz 251 half-track is November 22 1941, but no other details are known (69/94/16).

Left Pause for a smoke for men of the 'Totenkopf' Division. Note bright scarf around neck of foreground figure (78/22/25).

Right Grenadiers of the Leibstandarte-SS 'Adolf Hitler' in 1941 (78/22/19).

Far right Bringing up supplies to a 'Totenkopf' unit trench (78/22/24).

Below right The key, shield and oakleaves of the Leibstandarte-SS 'Adolf Hitler' is clearly marked on the back of this truck, together with the tactical sign for a Panzer support unit. The truck's occupants are all warmly dressed in reversible winter clothing (73/99/70).

Below 'Das Reich' MG 34 gunner. Note NCO tresse around collar of background figure (78/22/18).

Early StuG III with short-barrelled 7.5 cm gun during the winter of 1941 (78/22/17).
Anti-tank crew, said to be of the 'Totenkopf' Division, with Pak 37 in whitewash snow camouflage (78/22/16).

SS grenadiers with PzKpfw IIIs on the vast white Russian plains (73/98/14).

SS Oberscharführer (right) with other NCOs wearing crude sheepskin jackets, winter 1941–1942 (69/143/11).

Above This StuG III crewman
from the 'Totenkopf' Division
wears the SS version of the
field-grey jacket and trousers for
self-propelled gun crews with
more rounded lapels than its
Army equivalent. His rank
appears to be Hauptscharführer.
The significance of the number
13 and letter 'S' on the StuG is
unknown (141/1283/11).

Above left Wespe 10.5 cm
self-propelled gun on PzKpfw
II chassis. The SS crewman on
the right wears the reversible
white/mottle uniform devised
for tank and SPG crews
(73/113/4).

Left Early Marder III of an SS
Panzerjäger unit, mounting the
Russian 76.2 mm gun on
PzKpfw 38(t) chassis
(73/98/12).

Right SS Marder III with crew
in reversible winter uniforms
(77/127/11).

Above SS PzKpfw III, SdKfz 251 and Tigers during a temporary thaw (73/93/36).

Above right Disabled Tiger I which has lost its nearside track but appears to be otherwise functional or else why should the commander have bothered to erect a 'tent' over his cupola? (458/77/12).

Right Although the cuff title on the foreground SS Rottenführer's arm is unfortunately illegible, these men almost certainly belong to the Leibstandarte-SS 'Adolf Hitler' (78/22/4).

Left Waffen-SS grenadiers waiting for a Russian attack. This shows the camouflaged side of the reversible winter clothing. Weapons include an MG 42 machine-gun and, in the background, a 20 mm flak gun deployed in the anti-personnel role (70/25/52).

Background photograph SS StuG III Ausf F with long-barrelled 7.5 cm gun in winter camouflage (84/3416/18A).

Left inset SS Tiger I on the march (458/79/6).

Right inset Tiger Is with mounted grenadiers of an unidentified SS unit (277/846/10).

The photographs of vehicles in this sequence are particularly interesting quite apart from their clarity because they are known to have been taken during February 1943 yet clearly the tanks display the alternative 'Das Reich' divisional device which has commonly been understood to have been introduced for the Battle of Kursk later in the same year.

Left 'Das Reich' Tiger I (571/1721/31).

Right A PzKpfw IV Ausf H with spaced armour and zimmerit anti-magnetic mine paste (571/1721/27).

Below right Rear view of 'Das Reich' PzKpfw IVHs (571/1721/21).

Below Two PzKpfw IVHs, the foreground vehicle with slightly battered side skirts, and Tiger Is in the background, all of SS 'Das Reich' (571/1721/26).

Left The mark on the side of this Tiger I's turret appears to be a scratch, not some unidentified tactical marking (571/1721/29).

Right Tiger I at speed (571/1721/18).

Below left The turret number 'S13' can just be discerned on the foreground Tiger here, while 'S33' is more legible on the rear of the background vehicle (571/1721/32).

Below 'Das Reich' PzKpfw V Panther taken at the same time. The foreground car carries a Luftwaffe (WL) number plate (571/1721/14).

Left Another 'Das Reich' Panther. Note absence of divisional markings on PzKpfw Vs in general (571/1721/13).

Right Leibstandarte-SS 'Adolf Hitler' PzKpfw IIIs advance into Kharkov, March 1943 (73/113/10).

Below right SS 'Totenkopf' Division PzKpfw IV and grenadiers during the fierce fighting around Kharkov in March 1943. The commander, an Oberscharführer, wears the SS-pattern Panzer jacket with rank distinctions, arm eagle and cuff title, but a field grey field cap (73/113/18).

Below A tiny Leibstandarte-SS 'Adolf Hitler' badge can just be seen on the extreme top left-hand hull rear of this PzKpfw III, accompanied by SS grenadiers, in Kharkov (73/113/15).

Left PzKpfw III and grenadiers of the 'Totenkopf' Division in Kharkov (73/99/50).

Below right An officer of the Leibstandarte-SS 'Adolf Hitler' in Kharkov. He wears the 'old style' officer's cap without cords and one of the parkas which were issued to SS units at around this time (330/3021/27A).

Right Panthers with mounted grenadiers during the fighting of early 1943 (664/6759/30).

Below Tiger I and PzKpfw IVH outside Kharkov (277/843/14).

Finnish nurse in SS service (78/22/12).

SS NCOs (Unterscharführer in foreground) wearing parkas, Kharkov, March 1943 (73/114/36A).

Men of the Leibstandarte-SS 'Adolf Hitler' manhandle a 7.5 cm Pak 40 into action in Kharkov (73/84/55).

A hit for the crew of an SS Pak 38 in early 1943 (73/98/34).

SdKfz 251 outside the field dressing station of the Leibstandarte-SS 'Adolf Hitler' in Kharkov (73/100/4).

Above PzKpfw IVs and a captured T-34, SS 'Das Reich', spring 1943 (73/93/58).

Above right Grenadiers of the Leibstandarte-SS 'Adolf Hitler' outside Kharkov (78/122/35).

Left The SS combat soldier in action: not the well-groomed, elegant figure of popular imagination, but a swaddled figure mainly interested in keeping warm! (78/22/36).

Right Leibstandarte-SS 'Adolf Hitler' PzKpfw IVF2 outside. Kharkov (73/85/74).

Above PzKpfw III and SS grenadiers, probably of the
Leibstandarte-SS 'Adolf Hitler'
outside Kharkov (78/22/34).

Above left Knocked-out
LSSAH PzKpfw IVF2 in
Kharkov (330/3021/21A).

Left Top brass! From left to
right, SS-Brigadeführer
Hauser, commander of the 'Das
Reich' Division and later II SS
Panzer Korps; Ostendorff, rank
unknown at the time of this
photograph; and Klingenberg,
the 'Das Reich's much-
decorated recce commander
(78/22/31).

Right After the final victory in
Kharkov, a couple of SS grenadiers take a moment's break
(73/98/38).

Left LSSAH in Kharkov (78/20/0A).

Right Commander of a 'Das Reich' Tiger, a Scharführer, wearing the SS camouflaged tank crew overalls, during the Battle of Kursk in 1943 (73/80/48).

Below left The Battle of Kursk, largest armoured encounter of World War 2. Here a 'Das Reich' Tiger I, displaying the 'alternative marking' mentioned earlier, advances across the steppe (78/20/1A).

Below Well, whether we're winning or losing, these will come in handy . . . SS grenadiers relax during the fierce fighting around Kursk (73/95/14).

Inside a Tiger! These photographs were all taken within one Tiger I of Panzer Abteilung 502, SS 'Das Reich', in the summer of 1943. **Left** the commander in his cupola; **below** and inside; **above** the gunner – note sight on right of photograph.

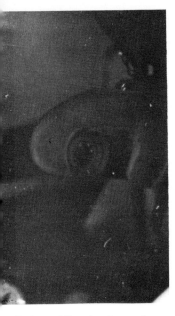

Below The loader, photo-graphed through his turret hatch; below right the hull machine-gunner/radio operator; and right the driver, complete with pipe (73/95/62, 68, 60, 58 and 66).

Left Probably, but not necessarily, posed, this picture purports to show the trust which existed between soldiers in the SS . . . and rather the guy on the right than me! (73/82/5).

Right Let's make hay, etc, or perhaps there aren't many Chinese laundries on the steppes . . . SS sniper during the Battle of Kursk (78/22/33).

Below So I called 'twos wild' and the (untranslatable German phrase) shot me . . . wounded SS grenadier during a respite at Kursk (73/89/28).

Above SdKfz 251 (foreground) which, interestingly, appears to have spare tank track links attached to its bonnet for added armour protection; and PzKpfw III, of the 'Das Reich' Division, during the Battle of Kursk (73/80/40).

Above right PzKpfw IVs with short-barrelled 7.5 cm guns, reputedly of 'Das Reich' although no markings are visible, during the summer 1943 battles (187/234/7A).

Right Very clear shot of a 'Das Reich' PzKpfw III moving up a road during the Battle of Kursk. Turret number is probably red, outlined white (125/257/24).

Left 'Totenkopf' Division NCO poses for the camera during a lull in the battle (73/94/64).

Left StuG III of unidentified SS unit during the same battle. It appears to have a criss-cross pattern of green and/or brown camouflage stripes across its basic yellow paint scheme (22/2944/2A).

Right Interesting shot of an SS infantryman with grenade adaptor attached to his carbine and entrenching tool stuck through his belt during the battle. Why the goggles? The black and white pennant on the left denotes an infantry battalion HQ (78/20/2A).

Below left Never mind the flowers, stick that shell in the breech . . . SS Pak 40 with several victories to its credit during the Battle of Kursk (73/85/36).

Below Brief respite for the crew of a 'Totenkopf' Division PzKpfw IV during the battle (78/22/23).

Left SS sniper with face mask (73/97/34).

Right Time for a quick kip for an SS grenadier during the battle: note straps for attaching camouflage to helmet (695/405/20A).

Far right SS sniper with face mask slung around his neck, Kursk, 1943 (73/82/7).

Below right Pak 40 at Kursk (73/92/88).

Below An SS NCO 'talking in' Luftwaffe support during the Battle of Kursk (73/88/86).

FAR RIGHT

PEWDER

ER NE WE Z EED

NEED → Gun Powder

Good shot of an SS grenadier firing his MP 40 from a command half-track (330/3023/17).

Left An SS NCO gives the order to advance. Note lack of all insignia, a common trend as the war progressed (actual date of photograph October 23 1943) (70/25/6).

SS tank crew reaming out the barrel of a PzKpfw IV (695/405/30A).

Above Signals vehicles of a motorised anti-tank unit, 'Totenkopf' Division, loaded on pallets prior to being transported by rail (73/82/73).

Above right Intriguing paint scheme on the side skirts of this StuG III from an unidentified SS unit (87/367A/7).

Right Excellent shot of a Leibstandarte-SS 'Adolf Hitler' Tiger I in zimmerit finish with its badge very clear to the right of the bow machine-gun. The radio operator/machine-gunner is wearing the SS tank crew camouflaged overalls, black Panzer field cap and goggles, while the officer perched on the turret appears to be wearing a motorcyclist's coat and 'old style' field cap (738/267/18).

Left Time for a wash and shave in between engagements for the crew of this SS Tiger I (461/216/32A).

Above SS MG 34 crew in an earthwork bunker (73/88/18).

Above right Heavy 15 cm sFH 18 with SS detachment (73/95/8).

Left SS radio operator. The arm eagle, worn against regulations on the camouflage tunic, is particularly clear (73/115/7).

Right 'Totenkopf' motorcyclists with an unidentified ally (73/82/35).

PREVIOUS SPREAD

Background photograph A grenadier from the 'Totenkopf' Division a moment after firing a grenade from his rifle attachment (78/22/22).

Top inset A quick lunch for an SS radio operator (73/101/61).

Bottom inset 'Das Reich' grenadiers during a momentary pause (78/22/30).

Bread by bike! Supplies brought to a front-line SS unit in the sidecar of a motorcycle (73/89/52).

Loading the 1,000th shell into the breech of an SS 10.5 cm leFH 18 (73/92/46).

First aid for a lightly wounded member of the 'Totenkopf' Division (78/22/21). no battle wound is light?
Below left 'Totenkopf' Division communications trench . . . somewhere in Russia (73/94/60).
Below right SS grenadier in action. Note bayonet attached to rifle (73/101/17).

Above 'Hohenstaufen' Division Hummel being loaded on to a flat car; note number plate, unusual on most AFVs (297/1708/3A).

Above left An early StuG III of the 'Florian Geyer' Division (see slogan on superstructure side) with two SS grenadiers from a mortar detachment in the foreground (73/113/5).

Left Good close-up of two crew members of a Hummel SPG from SS Division 'Hohenstaufen', both wearing the SS version of the field-grey SPG crew jacket (297/1707/32).

Right SS infantry inside an SdKfz 251: note variety of stores strapped to the vehicle's sides (73/113/3).

Background photograph Schwimmwagens of an SS motorised recce unit fording a river (73/114/37A).

Left inset Heavy going through the mud for this supply truck of the 'Wiking' Division, which also bears the 'K' of von Kleist's Panzergruppe (78/22/5).

Right inset StuG III and SS personnel in a Russian village (726/219/39).

Above Communications trench of the 'Polizei' Division showing the rank insignia of an Unterscharführer particularly clearly (694/305/9A).

Above left Infantry and Panzer officers of the 'Wiking' Division in 1944. The cords on the Panzer officer's cap appear to have been made for someone with a head two sizes larger! (74/43/34).

Left Summer 1944, and an SS NCO surveys the battlefield from behind a disabled T-34 (239/2095/7).

Right Excellent portrait shot of a rather self-satisfied looking Sturmbannführer, possibly from SS Gebirgs-Division 'Nord' (77/127/16).

Right Letter from home for a 'Wiking' Division Sturmann (centre), eagerly shared by a grenadier (left) and a Panzer Rottenführer (right), the latter interestingly wearing field grey trousers with his black Panzer jacket (78/22/2).

Below right An SS Untersturmführer (centre) of the 'Totenopf' Division reading a telegram with an Oberleutnant from the 228th Infantry Regiment, summer 1944 (24/3535/32).

Left and below Unusually, a divisional device – that of the 'Totenkopf' Division – can be seen on the bow plates of these Panthers in southern Russia (695/419/2A and /3A).

'Wiking' Division Panthers in
the Warsaw vicinity, 1944
(695/420/15, 73/103/70 and
77/138/34A).

Left Maintenance work on a 'Wiking' Division Tiger outside Warsaw, 1944; the one-piece camouflaged tank overall is clearly shown here (695/405/31A).

Right Generaloberst Dietl (left) during a visit to SS-Gebirgs-Division 'Nord' with Brigadeführer Kleinheisterkamp (right) (78/22/11).

Far right Unshaven SS grenadier, said to be of the Leibstandarte-SS 'Adolf Hitler', with Panzerfaust, a somewhat faded but very atmospheric photograph (709/304/2).

Below right Another shot from the same sequence showing a well-laden SS grenadier in a fur hat alongside a whitewashed PzKpfw IVH (709/304/7).

Below SS Hetzer and motorcycle combination, also in southern Russia (715/213A/25).

Above One of the very rare Bundesarchiv pictures from the tail end of the war, showing a Waffen-SS StuG III in Hungary on January 22 1945 (70/25/4).

Above right PzKpfw IVH of either the 'Totenkopf' or 'Wiking' divisions in 1944 (695/406/2A).

Right Tiger I, again belonging to either the 'Totenkopf' or 'Wiking' Divisions, in 1944 (695/406/15A).

Left Good portrait shot of a 'Totenkopf' Division tank commander in 1944 (695/406/16A).

Inset left A break in the terrible fighting against the Warsaw rebellion for these two 'Wiking' Division grenadiers (695/426/21).

Inset right SS grenadiers in Warsaw, displaying a wide variety of clothing and equipment: note spare machine-gun barrel containers on the backs of the two figures in the right foreground (696/426/22).

Background photograph Dramatic view of Nebelwerfers being launched over the ruins of Warsaw by an SS battery (696/426/20).

APPENDIX

Establishment strength of an SS Panzer Division in 1944

Unit	Men	Machine-guns	Mortars*	Flak Heavy	Flak Light	Artillery† SP	Artillery† Towed	Tanks Pz IV	Tanks Pz V	Motor cycles	Other vehicles
Div HQ	141	0	0	0	0	0	0	0	0	8	32
HQ Coy	219	18	2	0	4	3	0	0	0	28	31
Pz Regt	1771	297	0	0	14	0	0	64	62	53	313
Pz Gren Regt‡	3242	322	32	12	0	6	0	0	0	53	313
Pz Art Regt	2167	121	0	0	0	18	36	0	0	88	527
Flak Abt	824	22	0	12	18	0	0	0	0	40	534
NblW Abt	473	18	18	0	0	0	0	0	0	16	181
StuG Abt	344	22	0	0	0	22	0	0	0	8	107
Pz Recce Abt	942	151	10	0	0	13	35	0	0	11	100
Pz Signal Abt	515	35	0	0	0	0	0	0	0	22	199
Pz Pi Abt	984	105	6	0	0	0	6	0	0	14	114
Div services	1885	86	0	0	0	0	0	0	0	52	212
										85	323

* Includes Nebelwerfers.   † Includes anti-tank guns.   ‡ Normally two per division.

(Figures taken from D. B. Nash, *Miniature Warfare*, Vol 2, No 6, July 1969.)

SS Panzer Korps in Russia*

I   Summer 1943 (Dietrich)
II   1943 (Hausser)
III   1943–1945 (Steiner)

IV   Autumn 1944–spring 1945 (Gille)
VI   1943–1945 (von Pfeffer-Wildenbruch, von Treuenfeld and Krüger)

* Excludes those ad hoc 'Korps' formed late in the war which really existed in name only.

SS ranks with approximate* Wehrmacht, British and US equivalents

Schütze	Schütze	Private	Private
Oberschütze	Oberschütze	Private	PFC
Sturmann	Gefreiter	Lance Corporal	Acting Corporal
Rottenführer	Obergefreiter	Corporal	Corporal
Unterscharführer	Unteroffizier	Lance Sergeant	Sergeant
Scharführer	Unterfeldwebel	Sergeant	Staff Sergeant
Oberscharführer	Feldwebel	CSM	Technical Sergeant
Hauptscharführer	Oberfeldwebel	Sergeant-Major	Master Sergeant
Sturmscharführer	Hauptfeldwebel	RSM	1st Sergeant
Untersturmführer	Leutnant	2nd Lieutenant	2nd Lieutenant
Obersturmführer	Oberleutnant	Lieutenant	1st Lieutenant
Hauptsturmführer	Hauptmann	Captain	Captain
Sturmbannführer	Major	Major	Major
Obersturmbannführer	Oberstleutnant	Lieutenant-Colonel	Lieutenant-Colonel
Standartenführer	Oberst	Colonel	Colonel
Oberführer	Generalmajor	Major-General	Brigadier-General
Brigadeführer	Generalleutnant	Lieutenant-General	Major-General
Gruppenführer	General	General	Lieutenant-General
Obergruppenführer	Generaloberst	General	General
Oberstgruppenführer	Generalfeldmarschall	Field Marshal	General

* Approximate because, particularly in the NCO ranks, there is no real British or American equivalent in terms of seniority or responsibility.

Other titles in the same series

No 1 Panzers in the desert
by Bruce Quarrie
No 2 German bombers over England
by Bryan Philpott
No 4 Fighters defending the Reich
by Bryan Philpott

In preparation

No 5 Panzers in North-West Europe
by Bruce Quarrie
No 6 German fighters over the Mediterranean
by Bryan Philpott
No 7 Fallschirmjäger (German paratroops) in the Mediterranean
by Bruce Quarrie
No 8 German bombers over Russia
by Bryan Philpott

Plus many more!